THE WEAPONS ENCYCLOPÆDIA
TANK AIRCRAFT AFV SHIP ARTILLERY VEHICLES SECRET WEAPON

TWE-016 ENG

🇬🇧 MATILDA MK II TANK

THE WEAPONS ENCYCLOPAEDIA

EDITORIAL STAFF
Luca Cristini, Paolo Crippa.

ACADEMIC STAFF
Enrico Acerbi, Massimiliano Afiero, Aldo Antonicelli, Ruggero Calò, Luigi Carretta, Flavio Chistè, Anna Cristini, Carlo Cucut, Salvo Fagone, Enrico Finazzer, Björn Huber, Andrea Lombardi, Aymeric Lopez, Marco Lucchetti, Luigi Manes, Giovanni Maressi, Francesco Mattesini, Federico Peirani, Alberto Peruffo, Maurizio Raggi, Andrea Alberto Tallillo, Antonio Tallillo, Massimo Zorza.

PUBLISHED BY
Luca Cristini Editore (Soldiershop), via Orio, 35/4 - 24050 Zanica (BG) ITALY.

DISTRIBUTION BY
Soldiershop - www.soldiershop.com, Amazon, Ingram Spark, Berliner Zinnfigurem (D), LaFeltrinelli, Mondadori, Libera Editorial (Spain), Google book (eBook), Kobo, (eBoook), Apple Book (eBook).

PUBLISHING'S NOTES
None of unpublished images or text of our book may be reproduced in any format without the expressed written permission of Luca Cristini Editore (already Soldiershop.com) when not indicate as marked with license creative commons 3.0 or 4.0. Luca Cristini Editore has made every reasonable effort to locate, contact and acknowledge rights holders and to correctly apply terms and conditions to Content. Every effort has been made to trace the copyright of all the photographs. If there are unintentional omissions, please contact the publisher in writing at: info@soldiershop.com, who will correct all subsequent editions.

LICENSES COMMONS
This book may utilize part of material marked with license creative commons 3.0 or 4.0 (CC BY 4.0), (CC BY-ND 4.0), (CC BY-SA 4.0) or (CC0 1.0). We give appropriate attribution credit and indicate if change were made in the acknowledgments field. Our WTW books series utilize only fonts licensed under the SIL Open Font License or other free use license.

CONTRIBUTORS OF THIS VOLUME & ACKNOWLEDGEMENTS
Ringraziamo i principali collaboratori di questo numero: I profili dei carri sono tutti dell'autore. Le colorazioni delle foto sono di Anna Cristini. Ringraziamenti particolari a istituzioni nazionali e/o private quali: Stato Maggiore dell'esercito, Archivio di Stato, Bundesarchiv, Nara, Library of Congress ecc. A P.Crippa, A.Lopez, L.Manes, C.Cucut, archivi Tallillo. Model Victoria (www.modelvictoria.it), per avere messo a disposizione immagini o altro dei loro archivi.

For a complete list of Soldiershop titles, or for every information please contact us on our website: www.soldiershop.com or www.cristinieditore.com. E-mail: info@soldiershop.com. Keep up to date on Facebook & Twitter: https://www.facebook.com/soldiershop.publishing

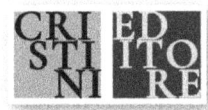

Title: **MATILDA MK II BRITISH TANK** Code.: **TWE-016 EN**
Series by L. S. Cristini
ISBN code: 9791255890164. First edition September 2023
THE WEAPONS ENCYCLOPAEDIA (SOLDIERSHOP) is a trademark of Luca Cristini Editore

THE WEAPONS ENCYCLOPÆDIA
TANK AIRCRAFT AFV SHIP ARTILLERY VEHICLES SECRET WEAPON

MATILDA MK II BRITISH TANK

LUCA STEFANO CRISTINI

BOOK SERIES FOR MODELERS & COLLECTORS

CONTENTS

Introduction 5
  - Development and design 5
  - Technical features 9

Operational use 23
  - Battle of France 1940 23
  - North Africa campaign 23
  - Minor campaigns 29
  - Other uses 30
  - After the Second World War 30

Camouflage and distinctive signs 41
  - European and metropolitan theatre colours 41
  - Middle Eastern and African theatre colours 42
  - Eastern colours 42

Versions of the vehicle 47

Data sheet 52

Bibliography 58

▼ Matilda Mk. II on display at the Base Borden Military Museum.

INTRODUCTION

The Matilda MK II, also known as the Matilda Senior, was an iconic British infantry assault tank of the Second World War, known for its extraordinary armour and its crucial role in the North African Campaign. Although it was relatively slow and had modest armament, its tough armour made it virtually invulnerable to most anti-tank guns of the time. It was born to replace the inadequate Matilda MK I. Its historical importance is reflected in its longevity, remaining in continuous service from the beginning to the end of World War II. Today, the Matilda II tanks preserved in museums and private collections represent a tangible reminder of an important era in the history of armoured vehicles. An icon of the courage and ingenuity of the Allied forces during the Second World War, they will forever remain a significant part of British military history.

DEVELOPMENT AND DESIGN

The origins of the Matilda tank can be traced back to the period following the financial crisis of 1929. Its first incarnation, known as the Mk.I Medium Tank, emerged in 1936, although it was immediately deemed unsuitable for actual battlefield operations. At the same time, in 1936, the A.12 specification was introduced, which called for a larger and better armed tank, taking inspiration from the earlier A.7 prototype. The A.12 differed significantly from its smaller counterpart in several aspects, including size, weight, transmission, armament and crew configuration.

The Matilda, initially introduced in 1937, had a relatively modest presence with only two units in active service when World War II broke out in September 1939. Subsequently, demand for this formidable tank grew, leading to a series of production orders from various manufacturers.

▲ The Matilda Mk I A11 E1 is considered the progenitor of the much more famous Matilda Mk II, which, apart from its name, inherits little else from this vehicle. Author's coloring.

Its development began in 1936 with the A12 specification, aimed at creating a cannon-equipped tank to replace the Infantry Tank Mark I A11, with which it curiously shared the name Matilda. Initially, the A12 was called the Matilda II or Matilda Senior to distinguish it from its smaller predecessor. However, after the abandonment of the Mark I variant in 1940, it acquired the universal name 'Matilda'.

The nomenclature of this tank, particularly with regard to the two tanks we are talking about, the Mark I and Mark II, underwent a rather complicated evolution: before 1941, various sources referred explicitly to the Infantry Tank Mark I as the Matilda, often with different name variations; but it was only after June 1941 that this tank received the official designation of Matilda. While the better-known Infantry Tank Mark II was similarly labelled as Matilda, with considerations for its reclassification as Matilda II.

Despite these complexities in nomenclature, it is crucial to emphasise that the Matilda tank and the Infantry Tank Mark I (A.11) differed significantly in both design and development, sharing only a vague visual similarity.

The first order for the new tank was placed with Vulcan Foundry, followed shortly afterwards by another contract awarded to Ruston & Hornsby. The combined efforts of these companies, together with the further involvement of John Fowler & Co. of Leeds, London, Midland and Scottish Railway at Harwich Works, Harland and Wolff and the North British Locomotive Company of Glasgow, led to the production of a truly remarkable total number of 2,987 Matilda tanks. This production extended until August 1943. The most important production took place in 1942, with no less than 1,330 units rolling off the assembly lines. Of these, the Mark IV model emerged as the most common variant of the Matilda.

However, the production process of the Matilda was not without its challenges and complications: one of them was the pointed nose of the tank that was cast as one piece. This, after initial removal from the mould, was thicker than it should be in some areas. Therefore, to avoid unnecessary additions to the weight of the tank, skilled workers were in charge of the meticulous process of grinding off the excess thickness. This task required precision and obviously added time to the production process.

▲ A Matilda Mk I of the 4th British Hussar Regiment in France in 1940. The image of this early Matilda, very eloquent, clearly reveals how cramped the interior and protruding the mechanical was... Wikipedia

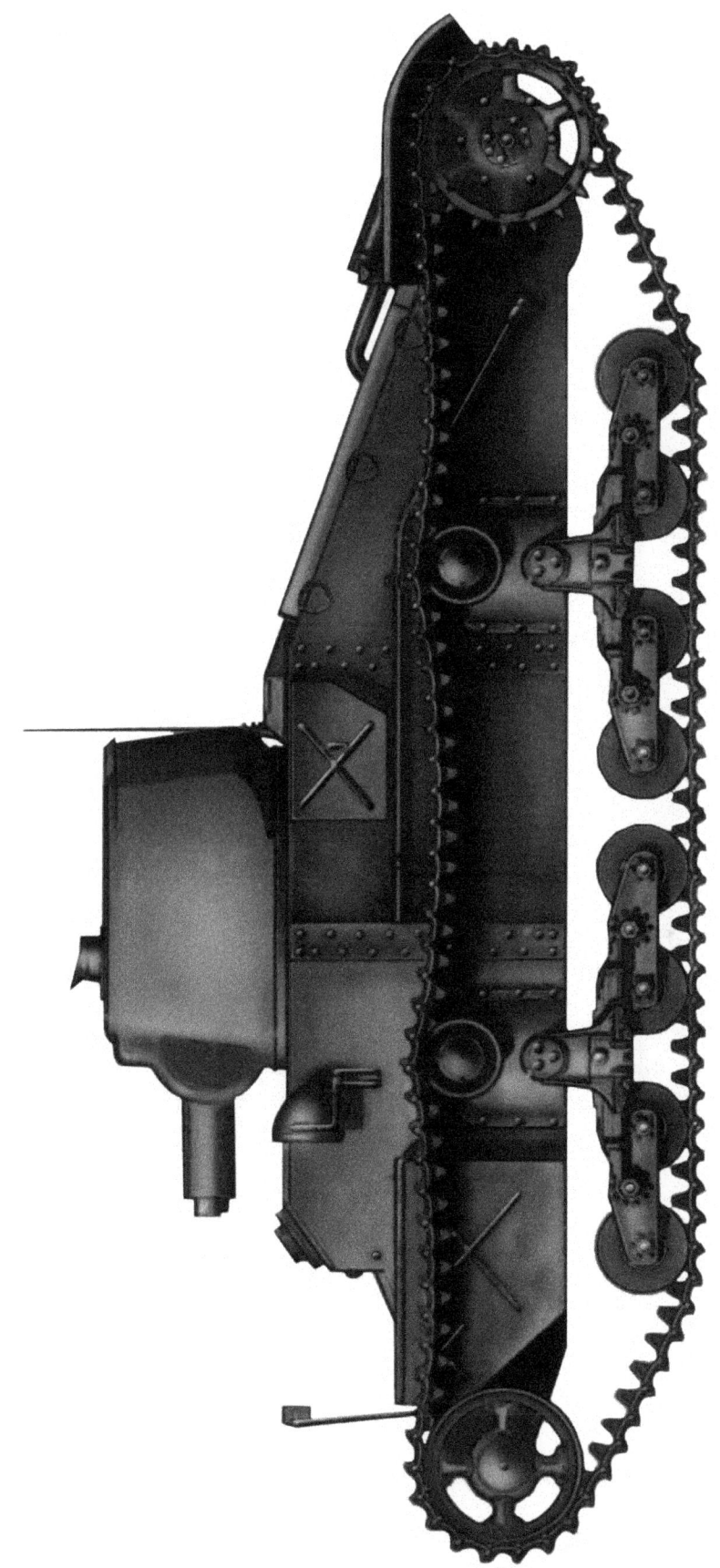

MATILDA MK I A.11 TANK OF THE 4TH RTR IN FRANCE, 1940

▲ British workers (two women are also seen) engaged in assembling a Matilda. Coloring by the author.

In addition, the complex suspension system of the tank and the multi-piece body side covers further contributed to the complexity of production, requiring specialised labour, which again resulted in longer production times for each unit.

Ultimately proving to be a relatively expensive and demanding vehicle to produce, besides other considerations, the tank ceased production in August 1943 after almost 3,000 units had been produced.

Despite these problems, the Matilda's extraordinary armour and capabilities made it a valuable *asset* to the British Army during World War II.

■ TECHNICAL FEATURES

The formidable British assault tank was distinguished by its impressive features and unrivalled armoured protection. Weighing around 27 tonnes, this tank boasted a level of vehicle protection unparalleled in its period. Armed with a 2-pound (40 mm) Ordnance QF anti-tank gun, housed in a versatile three-man turret, it was, at the time of its appearance, a formidable presence on the battlefield.

The turret, able to rotate a full 360 degrees, featured a hydraulic motor and manual operation, offering very good flexibility in aiming. The gun itself could be elevated in an arc that ranged from -15 to +20 degrees. However, one of the Matilda II's most notable shortcomings was the lack of a high explosive projectile available for its main gun. Although an explosive projectile was designed for the 2-pounder cannon, it was rarely used due to its low explosive charge. As a result, the tank often had to rely on its machine gun to effectively engage unarmoured targets.

In terms of layout, the Matilda II followed a conventional configuration. The driver's compartment occupied the front part of the tank hull, while the central combat chamber housed the turret. The engine and transmission were located in the rear. Access to the driver's position was typically through a single roof hatch, protected by a rotatable armoured cover that could be locked in the fully open or closed positions. In addition, a large escape hatch under the driver's seat served as an emergency exit. The driver enjoyed a direct vision window with a manually operated armoured shield and a single Mk IV periscope for use when the tank was closed.

▲ Beautiful view of a Matilda production workshop in Britain in 1941.

MATILDA MK II PROTOTYPE MODEL TANK, 1939

The Matilda's unique armour was a distinguishing feature of the British tank, with the slightly sloping front surface boasting a thickness of up to 78 mm (3.1 inches). The front plates, both upper and lower, were slightly thinner but strategically well angled for protection. The hull sides ranged from 65 to 70 millimetres (2.6 to 2.8 inches), while the rear armour, which protected the engine from the sides and rear, measured 55 millimetres (2.2 inches).

For this reason in particular, it differed from its contemporary rivals, such as the German Panzer III and Panzer IV tanks, which usually had hull armour between 30 and 50 millimetres (1.2 and 2.0 inches). Even the formidable Soviet T-34, known for its tough armour, had between 40 and 47 millimetres (1.6 and 1.9 inches) of armour, albeit inclined at 60 degrees. The Matilda's heavy armour, combined with its unique design influenced by Christie's concepts, earned it the nickname 'Queen of the Desert' in the early years of World War II.

However, this posed problems: the enormous weight of the chariot's armour had an inevitable cost in terms of mobility. Its average speed was limited to around 6 miles per hour (9.7 km/h) on desert terrain and 16 miles per hour (26 km/h) on roads. This snail-like speed was mainly attributed to a problematic suspension system and a relatively undersized engine.

The Matilda's power unit consisted of two six-cylinder AEC engines connected to a single shaft, a complex set-up that presented maintenance challenges. However, it did at least have the advantage of offering some redundancy, allowing the tank to continue running even if one of the two engines failed. The power of the engines was transmitted through an epicoilic six-speed Wilson gearbox, operated by compressed air.

The tank's cylindrical three-man turret was positioned on a ball-bearing ring mount, with a thick uniform 75 mm (2.95 inch) shield all around. Inside the turret, the pointer and commander sat in a scaled arrangement on the left side of the gun, while the loader occupied the right side. The commander could enjoy a rotating dome with a two-piece cover and a single Mk IV panoramic periscope installed in the

▲ Side view of a Matilda II in 1940/1941.

MATILDA MK II TANK OF THE 7TH RTR 1ST ARMY TANK BRIGADE, FRANCE, MAY 1940

▲▼ Above is a superb image of a Matilda II in the North African desert. Below a curious image, a British "Scammell" transport loads a Matilda already captured by the Germans and now recovered.

MATILDA MK II TANK IN FRANCE, MAY 1940

forward-facing access door. The same device was mounted in a fixed position in the turret roof, enhancing the pointer's situational awareness and target search capabilities. Loader access was through a single rectangular hatch in the turret roof on the right side. The turret also included an ammunition basket and featured an electric rotation system for normal operations, supported by a mechanically operated manual emergency mechanism.

The tank roof, including the turret roof and engine deck, maintained a constant thickness of 20 millimetres (0.79 inches). The overall thickness of the armour varied from IT.80 to IT.100.

The tank's suspension system was based on a Vickers design developed for the Medium C prototype in the early 1920s. It pivoted on five twin-wheel bogies on each side, with four of them coupled on swing arms with a common horizontal coil spring. The fifth bogie at the rear was suspended against a hull support. A vertical spring-loaded 'support roller' was positioned between the first bogie and the drive wheel to further help the tank overcome difficult terrain. Initially, the Matildas had return rollers, which were later replaced with more manageable tracking skids to facilitate production and field maintenance.

In terms of armament, the turret contained the main gun, with the machine gun positioned on the right inside a rotating inner shell. Turret rotation was achieved through a hydraulic system. The camouflage scheme of the tank was the result of a unique creative idea of Major Denys Pavitt of the Camouflage Development and Training Centre. It incorporated block colours, visually dividing the tank in half for greater camouflage performance through innovative patterns on the battlefield.

The design of the Matilda also incorporated unique features, such as the 'door bell' near the exhausts, designed to facilitate communication with infantry operating out of the tank.

Over time, some features evolved or were replaced, such as the transition from the configuration with three return rollers to the more manageable track shoe configuration and the replacement of the leather belts with a tubular metal structure on the turret.

▲ Prototype of the Matilda in 1939 during test runs.

▲ Various pictures of the Matilda II wagons in Africa; above: together with the Scamell transport.

▲ Matilda II in the BEF force in France in 1940, hit by a German tank catches fire. Above: Matilda in northern France, 1940.

MATILDA MK II OF THE 42ND RTR, 1ST ARMY TANK BRIGADE - LIBYA, NOVEMBER 1941

▲ A Matilda II destroyed in the middle of the desert. Despite the powerful armor, taking a hit to the tracks was lethal even for the desert queen. The advent then of German 88 pieces made all the difference.

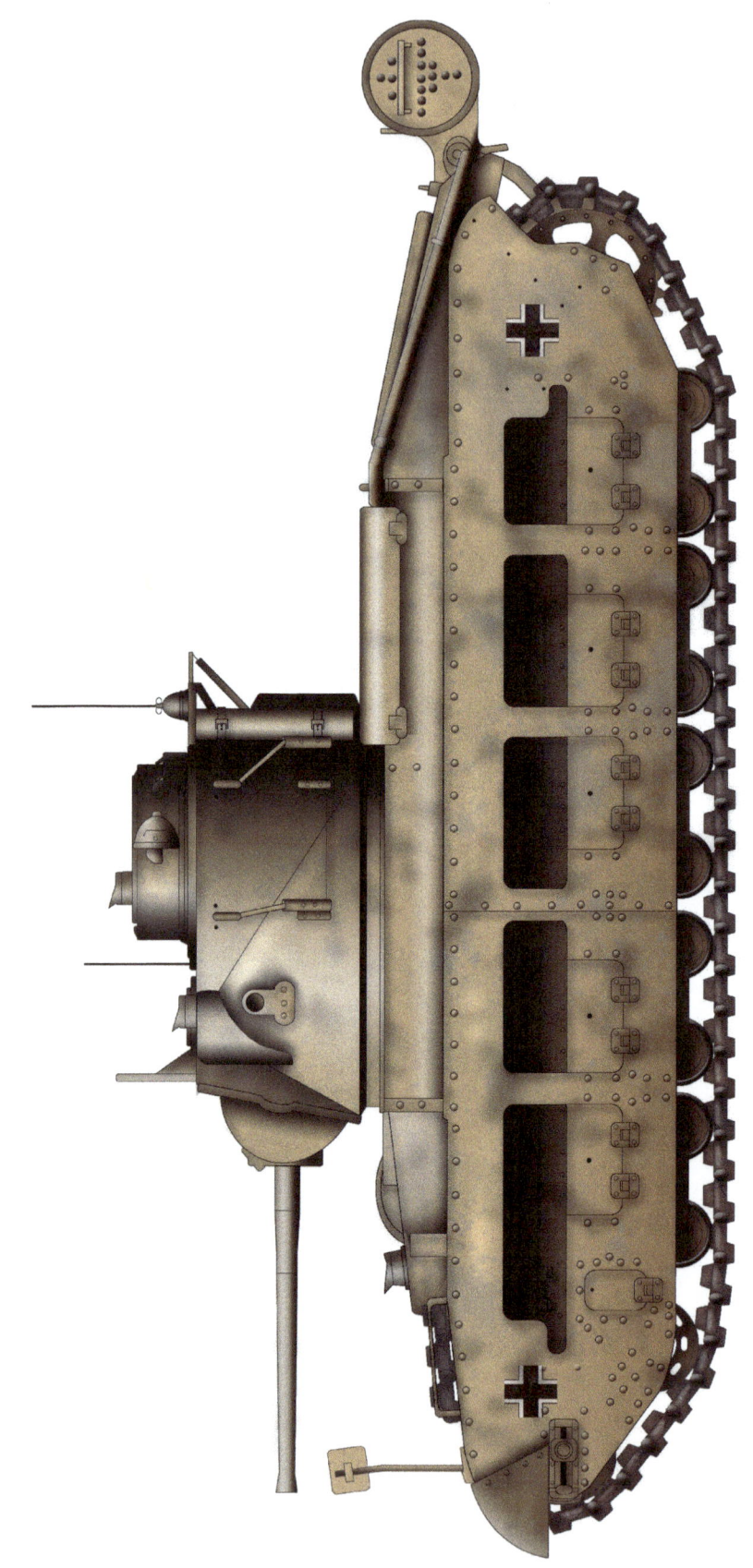

MATILDA MK II CAPTURED BY GERMAN TROOPS AND REUSED, LIBYA, BARDIA 1941

▲ A British Matilda II tank captured by the Germans who load it onto one of their transports.
▼ Another Matilda captured by the Germans (perhaps in Russia) and viewed by engineer troops.

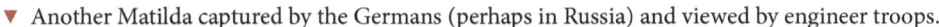

▲ The camouflage of the Matilda IIs, as in the case of this one preserved at the Bovington Museum, was very curious.

▲ A Matilda Tank II is loaded onto a transporter to be taken to the North African desert area of operations. Summer 1942.

OPERATIONAL USE

Entering operational service in 1939, with only two active examples at the outbreak of World War II in September, it was used extensively during the Desert War, particularly in North Africa, where, as already mentioned, it earned the nickname 'Queen of the Desert'.

■ BATTLE OF FRANCE 1940

The Matilda made its combat debut during the Battle of France in 1940. Of the British infantry assault tanks deployed, only 23 were Matilda IIs, the others being the smaller Matilda A11 tanks armed only with machine guns. Despite its 2-pounder gun, comparable to the guns of other tanks of the time, as already expressed, the Matilda II was known for its formidable armoured protection, which made it largely immune, though not invulnerable, to German anti-tank guns and guns in France. German 88 mm anti-tank guns proved to be the most effective measure against it. During the counter attack on Arras in May 1940, British Matilda tanks momentarily hindered the German advance, but suffered heavy losses. Eventually, many Matildas were abandoned or destroyed to avoid capture as the British retreated from Dunkirk.

■ NORTH AFRICA CAMPAIGN

After the evacuation from Dunkirk, the Matilda II tanks continued to serve with honour in the North African theatre. Their traditional combination of tough armour and modest firepower proved especially effective against Italian tanks, which were mainly equipped with light guns, so much so that the British tank earned another nickname: 'the Terror of Italian Tanks'. During the Second Battle of El Alamein, the Matilda II contributed significantly to the Allied victory, effectively impeding the advance of the Axis

▲ There were numerous Matildas that ended up in German hands, often even in excellent condition, like the one shown in the images and photographed by German officers.

MATILDA MK II OF THE 7ᵀᴴ RTR, IN LIBYA, JANUARY 1941

forces. The tank was also particularly valued for its ability to withstand the climate and desert terrain of North Africa, where other tanks could have serious mechanical problems. Its slow operational speed was less of a problem in a theatre of war characterised by wide open spaces. In addition, the British equipped it with continuous improvements such as a more powerful 2-pounder long-barrelled gun, which made it even more effective against enemy tanks.

North Africa 1940-1942: during Operation Compass, the Matildas of the British 7th Armoured Division wreaked havoc among the Italian forces. Up until at least the end of November 1941, the German army's combat reports indicated the difficulty in dealing with the Matilda. However, the Matilda's slowness and poor manoeuvrability eventually became problematic in desert warfare. When the famous Afrika Korps led by Marshal Rommel arrived, it got worse for the Matilda and it began to suffer increasingly heavy losses due to the 88 mm anti-aircraft artillery, which was extremely effective in the desert, and the more powerful anti-tank weapons. Despite all these new challenges, the Matilda played a crucial role in Operation Crusader, contributing to the liberation of Tobruk and the capture of Bardia.

Later, in North Africa: as the German army received more and more advanced tanks and anti-tank weapons, the Matilda's effectiveness diminished. Shooting tests conducted by the Afrika Korps clearly revealed vulnerabilities to various German weapons. Attempts to upgrade the Matilda eventually proved impractical due to the size of the turret. Therefore, the Valentine tank was introduced, which offered a faster and cheaper alternative, leading to the gradual retirement of the Matilda due to wear and obsolescence. By the time of the Second Battle of El Alamein in October 1942, there were only a few Matildas left in service, some of which were converted into sweeper tanks to clear the huge minefields placed by Axis forces across the desert.

▲ A Matilda II runs triumphantly back to its positions with a newly captured Italian flag.

▲ A non-Matilda Matilda... It is in fact a medium Italian tank camouflaged with plywood for the very purpose of not being targeted by enemy forces.

▲ A Matilda, already used by German forces, is recaptured, and its crew is made prisoners by New Zealand troops on Dec. 3, 1941 during Operation Crusader near Tobruk (author's coloring).

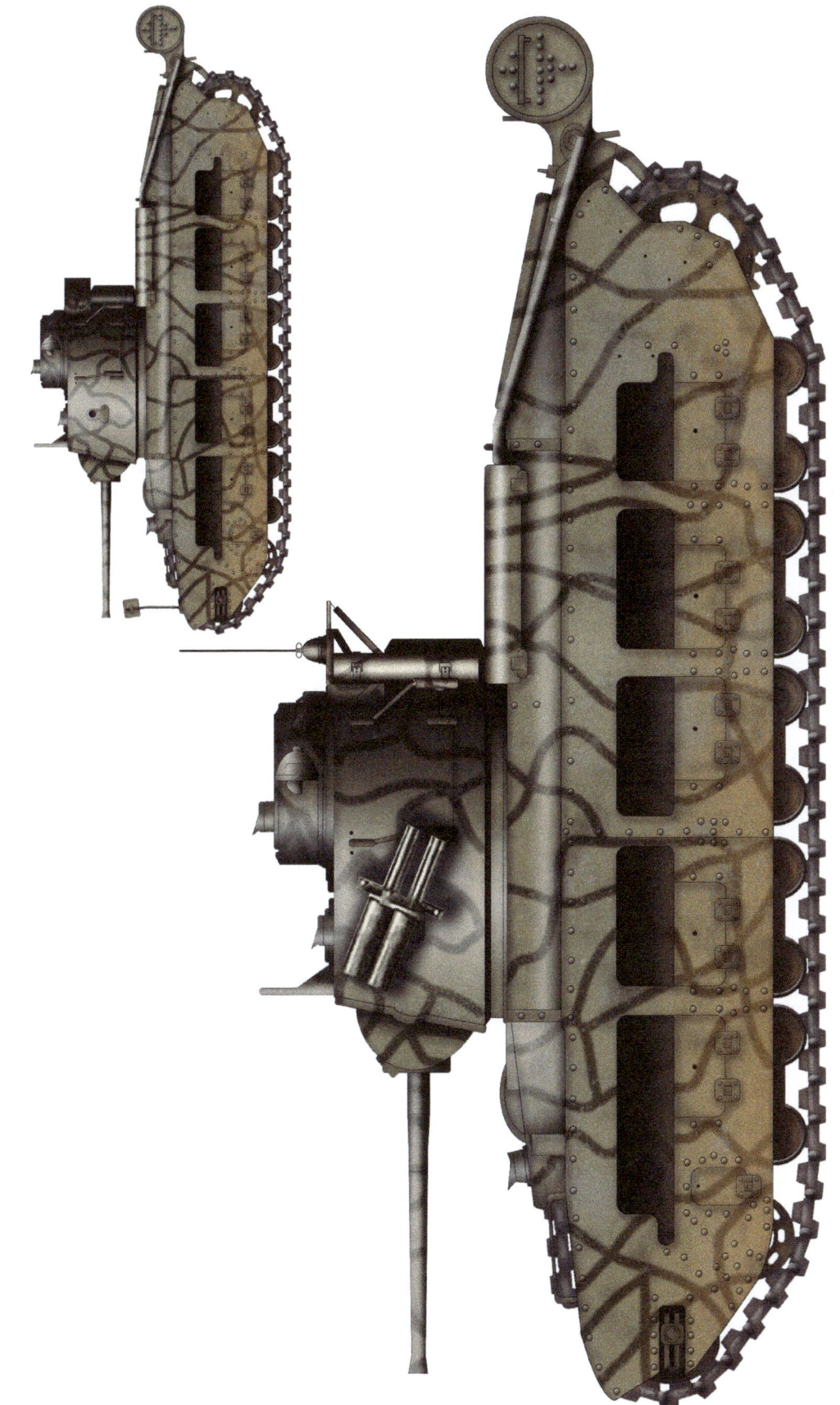

MATILDA MK II OF THE 4TH MALTA TANK INDEPENDENT, MALTA 1942

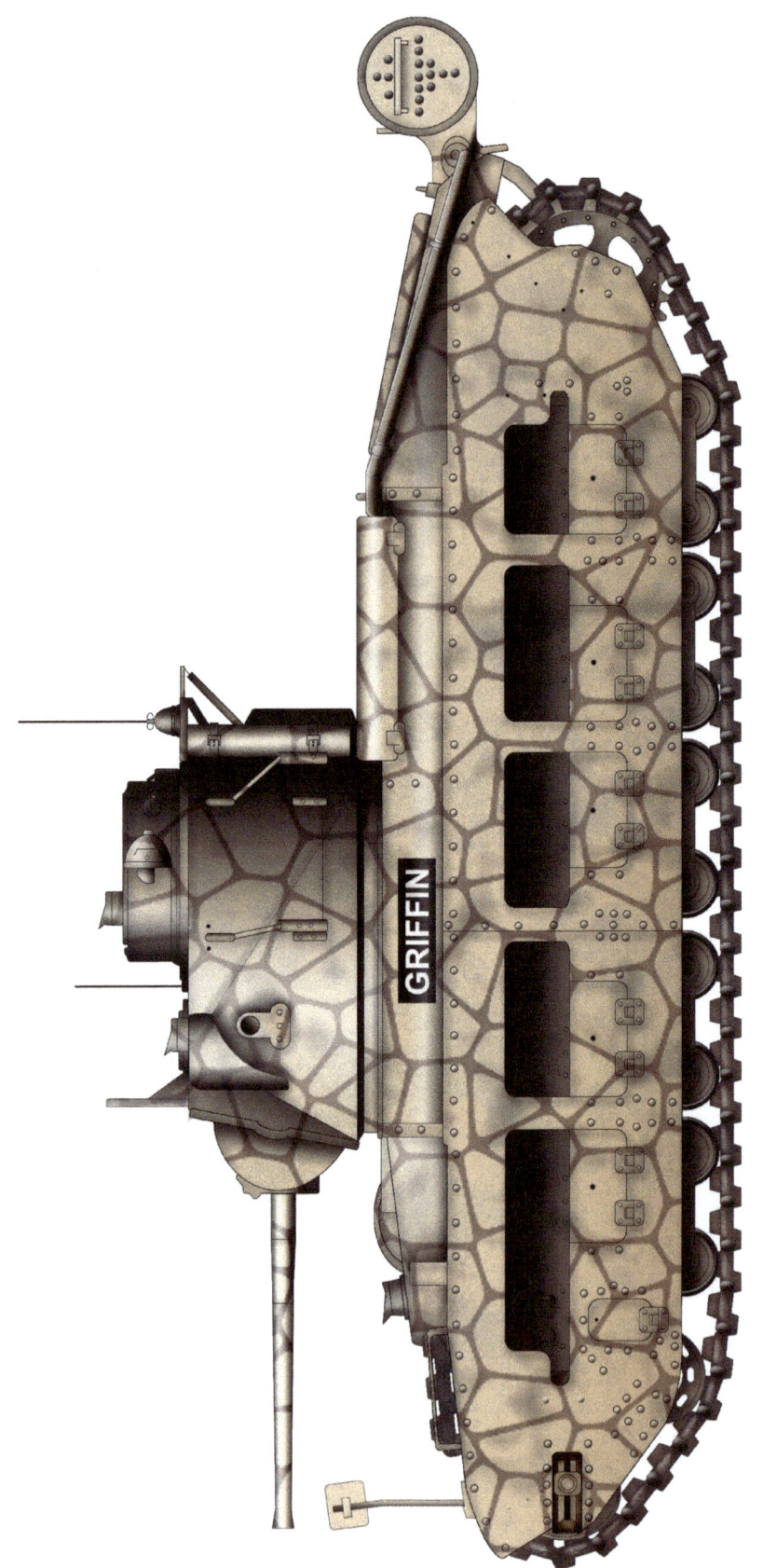

MATILDA MK III "GRIFFIN" OF THE 4TH MALTA TANK INDEPENDENT, MALTA 1942

MINOR CAMPAIGNS

In early 1941, the Matildas were deployed in the East African Campaign (in the fierce Battle of Keren), although the terrain severely limited their effectiveness. During the Battle of Crete, all Matildas present were lost in the fighting.

Australian deployment in the Pacific: the Australian Army received a total of 409 Matilda IIs from Britain and a further 33 Matildas as close support from New Zealand. These tanks were deployed in the Southwest Pacific, particularly in the Huon Peninsula, Bougainville and Borneo campaigns. Their heavy armour once again proved invaluable in jungle warfare. Some Matildas were modified for specific roles, such as the Matilda Frog, armed with a flamethrower, and the Matilda Hedgehog, capable of firing mortar shells.

Participation in Allied operations: the Matilda II continued to be used in other Allied campaigns, including operations in Greece, Syria, Iraq and Malaya during World War II. However, while continuing to prove its robustness and effectiveness, the Matilda II was gradually giving way to lighter and cheaper tanks such as the Valentine.

▲ Matilda II tank of the Independent Armored Regiment stationed on the island of Malta. Note the vehicle's curious camouflage, also clearly visible in the profile here on the left.

■ OTHER USES

Soviet deployment: the Red Army received 918 Matildas of the 1,084 sent to the USSR. The Soviet Matildas were mainly used during the Battle of Moscow and during 1942, but were criticised for their notorious slowness and reliability problems. Modifications were then made to improve traction, but most of the Soviet Matildas were put out of action or stopped by 1944.

Use of Matildas captured by the Germans: after Operation Battleaxe, the Germans repaired and used the captured Matildas, designating them as 'Infanterie Panzerkampfwagen Mk.II 748(e)'. These tanks were well regarded by the German users, but caused a lot of confusion in battle.

There are also mentions of the capture of some Soviet Matildas by the Romanians, although this is not widely documented.

■ After the Second World War

After the end of the Second World War, the Matilda II was withdrawn from active service, but continued to be used by some nations for training purposes or made available as surplus equipment. Many Matilda II tanks were scrapped or given to Allied countries after the conflict.

Although no Matilda IIs remain in operational service to this day, several examples have been preserved in museums and private collections around the world. These vintage tanks continue to bear witness to their historical importance and their unique characteristics in comparison to World War II armoured vehicles.

Egyptian use: Egypt employed the Matildas against Israel during the 1948 Arab-Israeli War.

▲ Matilda II Mk.II 748(e) captured and redeployed by German Afrika Korps forces.

MATILDA MK II "BEUTEPANZER" REUSED BY THE GERMANS IN LIBYA, 1942

▲ A Matilda II with the gritty A.27 turret and a more powerful gun. Vehicle named Black Prince.

▲ Russian Matilda knocked out by German panzers.

▲ An Australian Matilda version Frog flamethrower in the Indonesian countryside in 1945.

▲ Australian Matilda landed at Toko Beach in 1945.

▲ View of the British Matila Mk II tank from above.

MATILDA MK II CS OF THE 6TH ARMOURED DIVISION, GREAT BRITAIN, SUMMER 1942

▲ An Australian Matilda II armed with a 9th Armoured Regiment howitzer major during the Battle of Tarakan in May 1945.
▼ The Australian Matilda rocket launcher known as the "Hedgehog".

▲ The Matilda II was used extensively in the campaigns of Borneo and Indonesia. Puckapunyal Museum.

▼ Australian troops watch a Matilda cross a bridge during the New Guinea campaign.

▲ Front and back views of the Matilda Mk II tank.

MATILDA MK II CANADIAN ARMORED UNIT, GREAT BRITAIN, SUMMER 1942

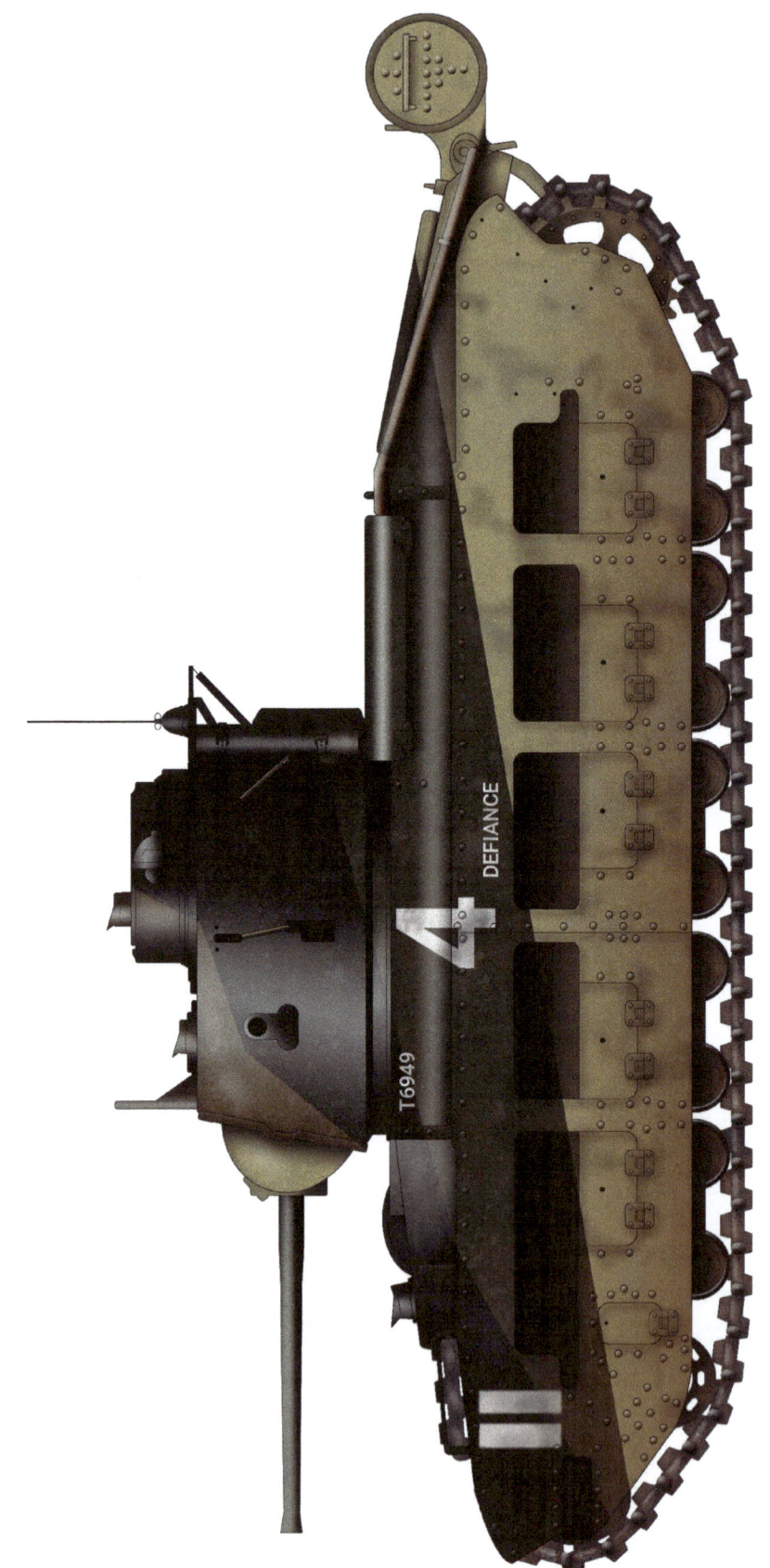

MATILDA MK IV "DEFIANCE" 4TH ROYAL A. REGIMENT, 8TH ARMY - EL ALAMEIN, OCTOBER 1942

CAMOUFLAGE AND DISTINCTIVE SIGNS

The background colours and camouflage tints of British military vehicles (AFVs) during the Second World War were determined by a series of Army Council (ACI) instructions and poured onto military training pamphlets (MTP), with specific general orders (GO) used in the Middle East. The paint was supplied to the units pre-mixed (PFU prepared for use) corresponding to two British standards: BS381C from 1930 and BS987C from 1942-45.

Contemporary photographs and the testimonies of veterans confirm that, with a few slight variations, these orders were mostly strictly adhered to but, as far as the models used were concerned, there were sometimes slight variations. The regulations, for example, provided for immediate application of the new regulations, however, even to exhaust old paint stocks, the old colour was often opted for

This led to the appearance of very curious colourings at times, often with interesting results involving all four basic colours.

■ EUROPEAN AND METROPOLITAN THEATRE COLOURS

Immediately after the end of the First World War, vehicles and AFVs continued to be painted as in 1914-18. In the 1920s, various colours were used, mainly the discounted browns, greens and greys. Officially these were called 'service colours', which are difficult to establish today.

However, in the early 1930s these colours were mainly a light khaki or greenish ochre.

The interiors of the vehicles were always a silver colour from the 1930s until around mid-1940, when glossy white was used for all. Soon after, and at least until early 1939, the service colour became a glossy *deep bronze green*.

In the first two years of the war, and more precisely from 1939 to 1941, horizontal/diagonal patterns of two different types of green were practised on military vehicles. The usual basic colour was khaki green with a dark green breaker called No. 4, or rarely light green No. 5, and alternatively *green* 3.

From the mid-1940s *dark tarmac* began to replace the two greens No. 4 and 5. Apparently, this choice was motivated by the need to preserve stocks of chromium oxide, an element needed to produce strong colours and a certain degree of infrared immunity. Between 1941 and 1942, the British standard camouflage colours (SCC) of the second British standard came into use until, once the old paint stocks were exhausted, both the greens and the *dark tarmac replaced them*.

However, shortages in supply and availability, caused by the scarcity of green pigment, caused the basic colour to be changed in many cases to brown, which in turn was darkened by a dark brown or alternatively black.

In the 1942-44 period, the diagrams introduced a new two-tone pattern using browns as per the regulations. The most common camouflage versions at the time were the *'foliage'* and/or *'dapple'* pattern.

In June 1943, the 1° Canadian Corps was instructed to repaint all vehicles in the basic *light stone* or *Portland stone* colour, with various areas of disturbance at the bottom of the body and cabin in black.

This was before deployment to North Africa to take part in Operation Husky in July 1943. The repainting included the addition of clear roundels on the roof to help the RAF recognise friendly vehicles.

In 1944-45, there was a switch to the use of *olive drab as the* new base colour, in order to eliminate the need to repaint US-supplied vehicles. From August 1944, therefore, except on vehicles already painted under the old regulations, *olive drab* became the formal base colour.

During the Italian campaign of 1943, many vehicles used the above-mentioned schemes, but others were painted according to the African-Middle Eastern scheme that used a base colour of *'light mud'* with bold black or dark olive green patterns.

Many of these vehicles were then repainted and, eventually, most of the British vehicle fleet was standardised with the basic *olive drab* coating.

■ MIDDLE EASTERN AND AFRICAN THEATRE COLOURS

In July 1939, the regulations for this strategic sector specified a basic tone called *middle stone* with variations of *'dark sand'*. The tanks of the 6th RTC A9 began to use the *stone* hue and in May 1940 added dark sand patches. This scheme became common in Egypt in the summer of 1940. In 1940-41 the vehicles were painted in three tones of *light stone* or *Portland stone* as a base colour with diagonal stripes and additions of *silver grey* and *slate* or *green* 3 used in different variations. A scheme used in Sudan included light *stone* or *Portland stone* with light brown-purple instead of silver grey, and *light stone* No. 61 instead of slate for the same model.

The two-tone pattern based on 'Caunter' and used in Greece in April and May 1941 was obtained by using *light stone* or slate or some other unknown colour. Light violet-brown, in short, was used exclusively in Sudan. In December 1941 the use of the two *stone* colours was still imposed, but only a possible third colour was added for camouflage. At first it appeared that slate-coloured camouflage was chosen, but later more and more vehicles with green or silver-grey camouflage or even brown were noticed. Various departments and brigades strove to choose a camouflage that would distinguish them from each other. This continued until October 1942, when a Camcolor range of water-based colours was developed for all camouflage purposes.

From October 1942 a new counterorder: all previous designs were cancelled to be replaced by new standardised designs for certain AFV types and vehicle classes.

The new colours that appeared on the horizon were a basic tone of *desert pink* with a disruptive pattern in *dark olive green*. Black, very dark brown and dark slate were the alternative variables.

These new patterns began to appear on Shermans, Grants, Valentines, Crusaders, and Stuarts; while Churchill tanks, painted in the UK with *light stone*, featured a red-brown pattern in the Crusader motif. Since *desert pink* was a new colour, *light stone* continued to be used on existing vehicles. *Desert pink* was then used alone as a single tone on vehicles without tactical value. From April 1943, the regulation was again cancelled and new models issued with new colours for use in Tunisia, Sicily, Italy and throughout the Middle East. The basic tone became *'light mud'* with black or other in bold patterns used for camouflage. Finally, in 1944, European colours and patterns also predominated in Middle Eastern vehicles.

■ EASTERN COLOURS

Until 1943, the vehicles appear to have conformed to UK standards. There are colour pictures of military vehicles in Singapore in *khaki green* and *dark tarmac*. In early 1943, *jungle green* was introduced to be used as the only general colour. But in 1944, *dark drab* also appeared. In 1944 there was a range of colours for camouflage purposes issued by SEAC in Ceylon (now Sri Lanka), but there is no evidence that any of these were intended as a disruptive colour. From 1943 to 1945 there was only one general base colour.

MATILDA MK II VARIANT WITH 76 MM CANNON COMMAND TANK VERSION - LIBYA 1942

▲ The Matilda rocket launcher studied by the Australian military and used in Borneo and Indonesia.

▼ A curious Matilda, called Canal Defence Light and appropriately named Dover...

MATILDA II MK IV IN RED ARMY SERVICE - DEFENSE OF LENINGRAD, 1942

MATILDA MK II TANK

MATILDA MK II CS IN SERVICE WITH THE SOVIET 5TH MECHANIZED CORPS 68TH ARMY RUSSIA, 1943

VERSIONS OF THE VEHICLE

Production of the Matilda tank chassis saw several adaptations and derivatives, each designed for specific purposes and roles:

- **Infantry Tank Mark II (Matilda II)**: the original Matilda tank equipped with a Vickers machine gun.
- **Infantry Tank Mark II.A (Matilda II Mk II)**: this variant replaced the Vickers machine gun with a Besa machine gun.
- **Infantry Tank Mark II.A. (Matilda II Mk III)**: featured a new Leyland diesel engine to replace the AEC engines.
- **Infantry Tank Mark II (Matilda II Mk IV)**: Improved version with higher performance engines, rigid mounting and no lamp in turret.
- **Matilda II Mk IV Close Support (CS)**: variant equipped with a 3-inch (76 mm) QF howitzer capable of firing explosive projectiles or smoke. Used for direct fire.
- **Infantry Tank Mark II (Matilda II Mk V)**: this version featured an improved gearbox and the use of a Westinghouse air servo.
- **Matilda Baron I, II, III, IIIA**: Matilda experimental frame with chain mines, never used operationally.
- **Matilda Scorpion I/II**: Matilda chassis equipped with a mine chain for demining operations, used in North Africa, including during the Battle of El Alamein.
- **Matilda II CDL/Matilda V CDL (Canal Defence Light)**: a late conversion with a cylindrical turret containing a powerful searchlight and BESA machine gun. Used to disorient and confuse the enemy at night...

▲ Matilda II flamethrower version of the 1st Australian Army, used in Borneo, June 1940. Puckapunyal Museum.

- **(Prototype) Matilda with A27 turret**: Matilda II modified with a 6-pounder Ordnance QF gun in an A27 turret. Only one prototype was produced.
- **(Prototype) Matilda II 'Black Prince'**: a radio-controlled prototype designed to detect anti-tank gun positions.

URSS:
- **Field modification of the Matilda Mark III with 76 mm ZiS-5 cannon**: a Matilda Mk. III supplied to the USSR was converted with a 76.2 mm ZiS-5 cannon, but this modification proved unsuccessful due to space limitations.

Australia:
- **Matilda Frog**: a Matilda flamethrower tank camouflaged to resemble a normal tank. Equipped with a flamethrower in place of the main gun, these tanks were active in Borneo and were considered effective.
- **Murray and Murray FT**: similar to the Frog but with a larger turret fuel tank, they used cordite instead of compressed air as propellant for the flamethrower. They never entered into action.
- **Matilda Tank-Dozer**: a bulldozer tank with a hydraulically driven bulldozer blade, mainly used to remove road obstacles and wooded areas.
- **Matilda Hedgehog**: Officially known as the 'Matilda Projector, Hedgehog, No. 1 Mark I', this variant featured a 7-chamber Hedgehog spigot mortar in an armoured box at the rear of the hull. The mortar was used to bomb enemy bunkers and was declared a complete success during testing, but was not used operationally before the end of the war. These various modifications and derivatives demonstrated the versatility of the Matilda chassis for specialised roles and specific war requirements.

▲ Matilda II CS supplied to the Red Army and now preserved in the Kubinka Museum in Russia.

▲ Matilda flamethrower Frog. Far East 1944.

▲ Matilda II tank as a deminer in the African desert.
▼ Another version of the Matilda II tank as a deminer.

🇬🇧 MATILDA MK II TANK

▲ Matilda II Bulldozer number 6940 ('Minstrel') shows its full power at Morotai, Indonesia June 9, 1945 - Courtesy by Australian War Memorial.

▼ Another Matilda Bullzdozer preserved in a museum in Cairn.

MATILDA II MK IV DEMINER VERSION - NORTH AFRICAN DESERT, 1943

DATA SHEET	
	Matilda II
Length	5720 mm
Width	2510 mm
Height	2610 mm
Date of entry/exit into service	1938/1944
Weight in combat order	27 t
Crew	4 (commander, driver, servant and gunner)
Engine	2x Leyland E148 & E149 6-cylinder diesel 95 hp engine
Maximum speed	24 km/h on road 13 km/h off road
Autonomy	112 km on road, 80 off road
Maximum slope	27
Armor thickness	From 15 to 78 mm
Armament	2-Pdr QF (40 mm/1.575 in), 94 shots available on board Besa 7.92 mm machine-gun, 2925 rounds available on board
Production	2987 units

▼ Matilda II standard in the early 1939-40s.

MATILDA II BULLDOZER VERSION 1ST ARMORED BRIGADE - BALIKPAPAN (INDONESIA), 1945

▲ Matilda II "Hedgehog" version of the Australian Army loading bullets into the launcher.

▼ Another image of Australian Army "Hedgehog" version Matilda wagon with multiple launchers placed on the rear of the wagon. This is the famous Bull Pup whose profile is on page 56.

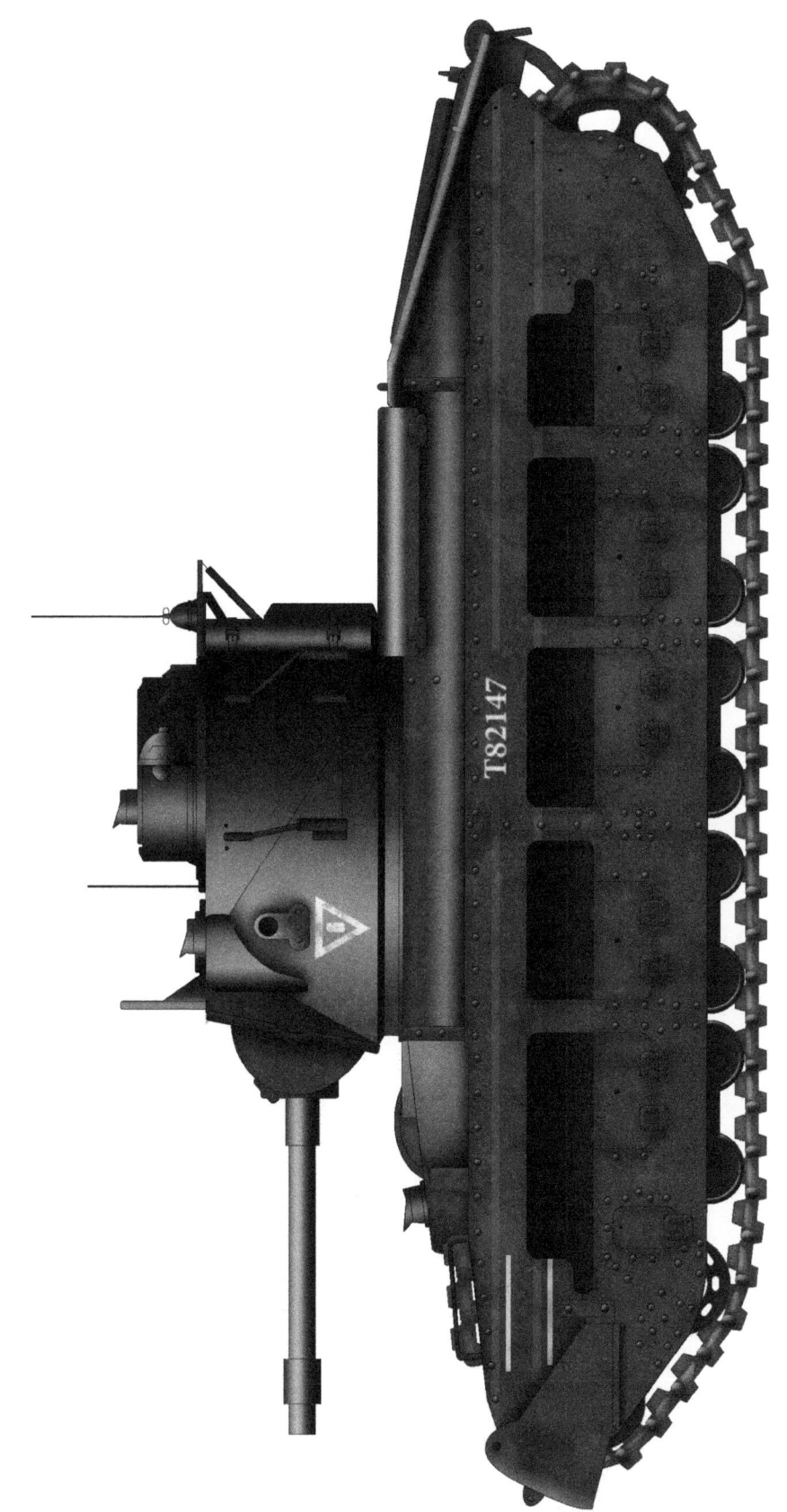

MATILDA II FLAMETHROWER VERSION 1ST AUSTRALIAN ARMY - BORNEO, JUNE 1945

MATILDA II "BULL-PUP" VERSION "HEDGEHOG" AUSTRALIAN ARMY - FAR EAST, 1945

MATILDA II AUSTRALIAN 29TH ARMOURED REG. - BATTLE OF TARAKAN, BORNEO 1945

MATILDA MK II TANK

BIBLIOGRAPHY

- Tim Bean, Fowler, Will, *Russian Tanks of World War II Stalin's armoured might,* Ian Allen publishing, 2002, ISBN 0-7110-2898-2.
- David Fletcher e Peter Sarson, *Matilda Infantry Tank 1938–45 (New Vanguard 8),* Oxford, Osprey Publishing, 1994, ISBN 1-85532-457-1.
- Thomas L. Jentz, *Tank Combat in North Africa: The Opening Rounds, Operations Sonnenblume, Brevity, Skorpion and Battleaxe, February 1941 - June 1941,* Schiffer Publishing Ltd, 1998, ISBN 0-7643-0226-4..
- *Britain's Matilda tanks, su WWII Vehicles, Tanks and Airplanes.*
- Boyd, David, *Matilda Mk II Infantry Tank (A.12),* su WWII Equipment, 31 dicembre 2008.
- Chamberlain, Peter; Ellis, Chris (1981), *British And American Tanks Of World War II (Second US ed.),* Arco, ISBN 0-668-04304-0
- Fletcher, David (1989). *The Great Tank Scandal: British Armour in the Second World War - Part 1.* HMSO. ISBN 978-0-11-290460-1.
- Hill, Alexander (2007). "British Lend Lease Aid and the Soviet War Effort, June 1941 – June 1942". The Journal of Military History.
- Kiński, Andrzej (2002). *"Czołg piechoty A 12 Matilda cz. 1"* [Infantry tank A 12 Matilda pt. 1]. Nowa Technika Wojskowa [New Military Technology] (in Polish)
- Kiński, Andrzej (2002). *"Czołg piechoty A 12 Matilda cz. 2"* [Infantry tank A 12 Matilda pt. 2]. Nowa Technika Wojskowa [New Military Technology] (in Polish)
- Murphy, W. E. (1961). Fairbrother, M. C. (ed.). *The Relief of Tobruk. Official History of New Zealand in the Second World War 1939–45* War History Branch.
- Orpen, Neil (1971). *War in the Desert.* Cape Town: Purnell. ISBN 978-0-360-00151-0.
- Pejčoch, Ivo; Pejs, Ondřej (2005). *Obrněná technika 6: Střední Evropa 1919–1945 (II. část) [Armoured Vehicles 6: Central Europe 1919–1945 (Part 2)]* (in Czech).
- Perrett, Bryan (1973). *The Matilda. Armour in Action.* Ian Allan. ISBN 0-7110-0405-6.
- Sebag-Montefiore, Hugh (2006). *Dunkirk: Fight to the Last Man.* Cambridge, MA: Harvard University Press.
- Tucker-Jones, Anthony (2007). *Hitler's Great Panzer Heist.* Pen and Sword Military. ISBN 978-1-84415-548-4.
- "Britain's Matilda tanks". WWII Vehicles, Tanks and Airplanes. Archived from the original on 24 March 2019.
- Anusz Ledwoch: *Tank Power vol. XLII, Matilda, Militaria 267.* Warszawa: Wydawnictwo Militaria, 2007. ISBN 978-83-7219-267-7.
- Tymoteusz Pawłowski. *Czołgi brytyjskie w Armii Czerwonej.* „Technika Wojskowa Historia". Nr 4 (22), s. 64–77, 2013. ISSN 2080-9743.
- Sears S.W., *World War II: Desert War,* New Word City, ISBN 978-1-61230-792-3.
- Jacek Solarz: *Tank Power vol. LXI, Matilda 1939 – 1945, Militaria 290.* Warszawa: Wydawnictwo Militaria, 2008. ISBN 978-83-7219-291-2.
- Stockings C., Bardia: *Myth, Reality and the Heirs of Anzac,* UNSW Press, 2009.

ALREADY PUBLISHED TITLES

ALL BOOKS IN THE SERIES ARE PRINTED IN ITALIAN AND ENGLISH

VISIT OUR WEBSITE FOR MORE INFORMATION ON THE WEAPONS ENCYCLOPAEDIA:

https://soldiershop.com/collane/libri/the-weapons-encyclopaedia/

TWE-016 EN

www.ingramcontent.com/pod-product-compliance
Lightning Source LLC
LaVergne TN
LVHW072122060526
838201LV00068B/4948